Cathy Heilig 95

Baby in a Basket

by Ruth Shannon Odor
illustrated by Helen Endres

THE CHILD'S WORLD

ELGIN, ILLINOIS 60120

Library of Congress Cataloging in Publication Data

Odor, Ruth Shannon.
　Baby in a basket.

　(Bible story books)
　SUMMARY: Brief text retells how the baby Moses was hidden in a basket placed among tall reeds along the river.
　1. Moses—Juvenile literature. 2. Bible. O.T.—Biography—Juvenile literature. [1. Moses. 2. Bible stories—O.T.] 1. Endres, Helen. II. Title. III. Series.
BS580.M6036　222'.1'0924 [B]　79-12092
ISBN 0-89565-086-X

Distributed by Standard Publishing, 8121 Hamilton Avenue, Cincinnati, Ohio 45231.

© 1979 The Child's World, Inc.
All rights reserved. Printed in U.S.A.

Baby in a Basket

The Biblical account of this story is found in *Exodus 1:15—2:10*.

"Come and see the new baby!" Father called to Miriam and Aaron. "It's a boy!"

The family gathered around the baby.

What a beautiful baby he was! He was perfect. He was strong. He was a very special baby.

The baby's mother, Jochebed (Jock-e-bed), smiled down at him. But after Miriam and Aaron had gone outside, there was a sad look on her face.

"Amram," she said to her husband, "what shall we do to keep the baby safe?"

"I don't know," said her husband. "The king has said that all boy babies of our people must be killed. The soldiers of the king are sure to find our son."

"We will pray to God," said Jochebed. "Somehow, some way, He will help us."

Miriam helped take care of the baby brother.

And often, Aaron came to play with him or just to stand and look at him.

"You are a very special baby," Jochebed said to her little son. "I will hide you. The soldiers must not find you."

So Jochebed kept the baby hidden in a part of the house where she thought he would not be found.

She fed him and bathed him. She played with him and sang to him. Oh, how she loved him!

The baby grew. Soon he was a month old. Then he was two months old, then three months old. His crying and cooing were louder. He could be heard all over the house. If the soldiers came looking for babies, they surely would find him.

"We can't hide him here in the house any longer," said his mother.

She thought and thought and prayed and prayed about what to do. Then she had an idea. Would it work? Yes, it might.

13

Jochebed took a basket. She covered it with tar and pitch, so that no water could get inside it. This made the basket like a little boat.

Carefully, she wrapped the baby in a soft, warm blanket. Tenderly, she laid him in the basket.

"Come, Miriam," she said. "Let's go to the river and hide the baby."

"On the river, Mother?" asked Miriam. "How can we hide him on the river?"

"Come and see," said her mother.

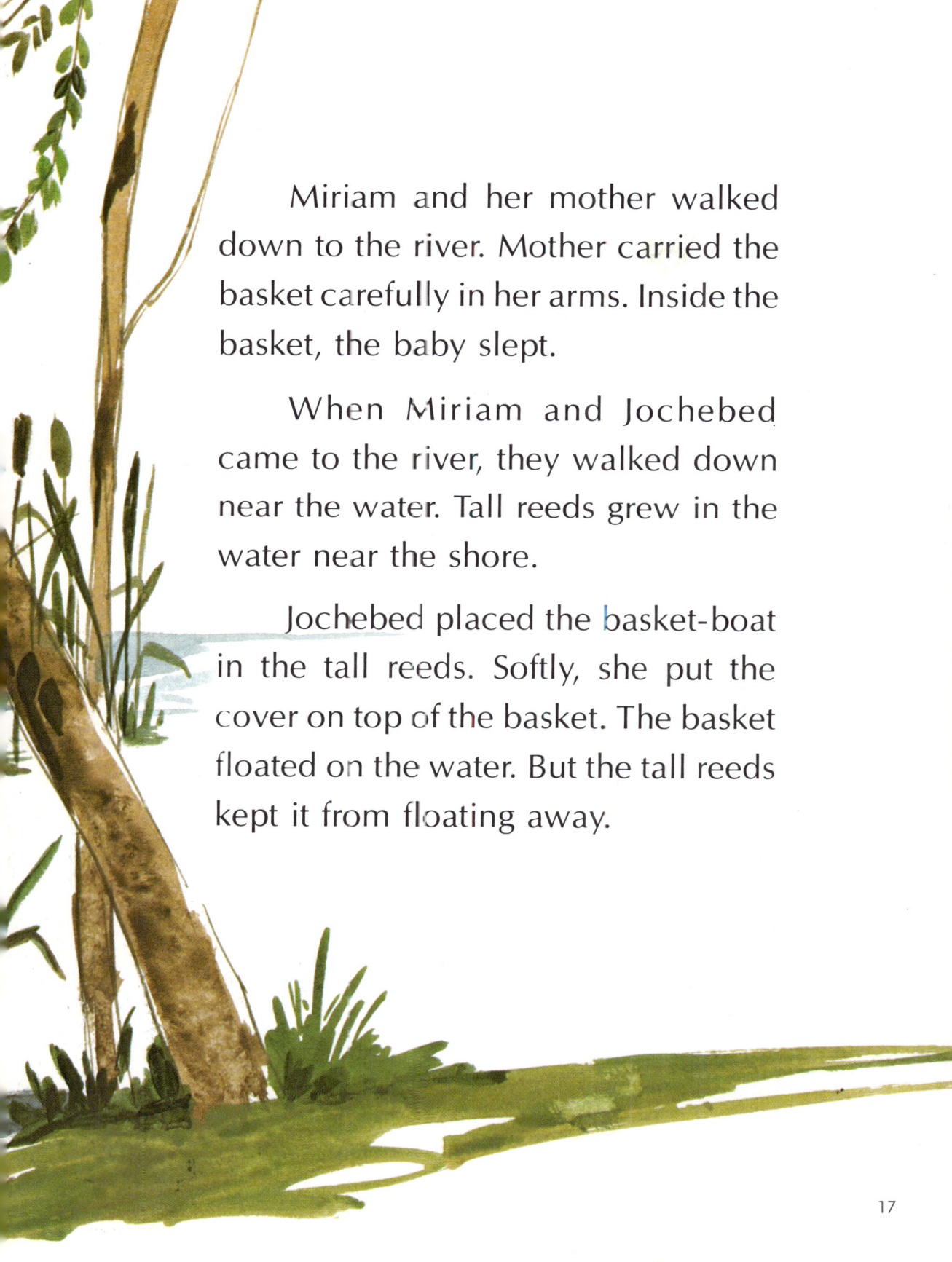

Miriam and her mother walked down to the river. Mother carried the basket carefully in her arms. Inside the basket, the baby slept.

When Miriam and Jochebed came to the river, they walked down near the water. Tall reeds grew in the water near the shore.

Jochebed placed the basket-boat in the tall reeds. Softly, she put the cover on top of the basket. The basket floated on the water. But the tall reeds kept it from floating away.

"He will be safe here," said Jochebed to Miriam. "Even if the soldiers search our house, they won't find him. But hide nearby and watch."

"I will, Mother," said Miriam. "Don't worry. I will watch and see that nothing happens to our baby."

Miriam sat down on the ground to wait and watch. White clouds floated across the blue sky. Birds flew in and out among the reeds. A soft breeze blew the waters.

And, in his basket-boat, the baby slept.

What was that? Miriam heard the sound of voices — women's voices talking and laughing. A group of women were walking down to the river. One was the Princess! Her servant girls were with her! The Princess was coming to bathe in the river!

"What will happen now?" Miriam worried.

As the Princess bathed in the water, her servant girls walked along the river bank.

Suddenly the Princess pointed. She had seen the basket-boat hidden in the tall reeds.

"What is that?" she said to her servant. "See? Over there. Get that and bring it to me."

The servant girl waded over to the basket-boat. She took it to the Princess.

The Princess opened the basket. And there she saw the baby boy. He was crying. Big tears rolled down his cheeks. The Princess felt sorry for him.

"This is one of the babies my father has ordered killed," she said.

The Princess saw that this was a very special baby. "No!" she said. "He can't be killed! I won't let him! I'll take care of him myself. I'll adopt him as my son!"

Miriam had heard. She came to the Princess. "Shall I go and find a woman of his people to take care of him for you?" she asked.

"Yes, go," answered the Princess.

Miriam ran home as fast as she could go.

"Mother! Mother!" she called. "Mother, come! Hurry! The Princess found our baby. She is going to adopt him. But for now, she wants a woman to take care of him. We can bring him back home again!"

"Thank You, God," Jochebed prayed. She ran with Miriam to the river.

The Princess handed the baby to his mother. "Take this baby and take care of him for me," she said. "I will pay you."

Jochebed took her baby into her arms. She held his soft, warm, little body against her once again. How happy she was!

At home, a happy family gathered around the baby. No one could harm him now. He was the Princess's adopted son.

One day, when he was older, he would go to the palace to live. He would be named Moses. He would be a great man. And one day, he would lead God's people out of this land to a land of their own.

But now, he was baby brother, safely home.